MW01658274

This is my house.

At my house I can hear…

BAM, BAM

see saw see

rap rap rap

Ssss Ssss

zing zing

Clunkety clunk clunk

At my house I can smell…

OOOoo

Sniffy

sniff

Whiff

sniff

mmmmm mmmmm

goooood

yummy

At my house I can taste…

Yum, yum

Sweeeeet

syrupy

tangy

Buttery

At my house I can see…

up Up UP

STRAIGHT

round

down down down

green

yellow

brown

At my house I can feel…

fluffy

smooth

warm

fuzzy

soft